TIME TRAVEL

Reader 4

Judy Garton-Sprenger
Philip Prowse

Published by Macmillan Education
Between Towns Road, Oxford, OX4 3PP, UK
Macmillan Education is an imprint of Macmillan Publishers Limited
Companies and representatives throughout the world

ISBN 1 405 00356 1

© Judy Garton-Sprenger and Philip Prowse 2002
Design and illustration © Macmillan Publishers Ltd 2002

All rights reserved; no part of this publication may be reproduced, stored in a retrieval system, transmitted in any form, or by any means, electronic, mechanical, photocopying, recording, or otherwise, without the prior written permission of the publishers.

Illustrated by Roger Wade Walker
Designed by Joanna Turner
Cover illustration by Roger Wade Walker
Cover designed by DW Design

Printed and bound in Colombia by Quebecor World Bogotá S.A.

2006   2005   2004   2003   2002
10   9   8   7   6   5   4   3   2   1

Contents

1	"Help!" Jack screamed	4
2	I don't believe you!	6
3	A magic gun	9
4	I've just seen a monster	11
5	It's dead now	13
6	If you don't get a job, I won't marry you	16
7	We've left Jenny behind!	18
8	This is amazing!	20
9	You're just in time!	22

1 "Help!" Jack screamed

Look at the pictures. Where are the people? What's happening?

It was a Friday afternoon in July in Boston, and the weather was sunny. It was very hot in the school science laboratory. Jack was 16. He wasn't very good at science but he loved playing soccer. He was on the school soccer team.

"We're playing today at 4:30," Jack thought and closed his eyes.

"Jack! Wake up!" It was Miss Williams, the science teacher, and she was angry.

"I'm sorry, Miss," Jack said.

"Come and see me at four o'clock!" Miss Williams said.

"Oh, but Miss," Jack said. "I have soccer at four thirty."

Miss Williams thought for a minute. "OK, come to the laboratory at nine o'clock tomorrow morning."

"But tomorrow's Saturday!" Jack said. "There's no school on Saturday."

"Yes, I know. But there is for you," Miss Williams said. "See you at nine."

Jack enjoyed the soccer game and his team won. The next morning he went to school on his rollerblades and found Miss Williams in the laboratory.

"Good morning, Jack," she said. "You can help me with this."

At the back of the laboratory there was something tall under a white cloth. Miss Williams took off the cloth. It was an old telephone booth!

"Don't look so surprised," she said. "I'm doing a project on Alexander Graham Bell."

"Who's he?" Jack asked.

"Never mind," the teacher said. "Take off your rollerblades. I want you to clean the phone booth."

It was hard work and Jack was soon bored. "Perhaps this old phone booth works," he thought. He picked up the phone and dialed his friend Tom's number: 156-6079. But when he dialed the first four numbers there was a loud explosion!

"What are you doing?" Miss Williams shouted. She opened the phone booth door. Suddenly there was another explosion, and the door closed. Jack and Miss Williams were inside the phone booth and everything went dark outside. Then the phone booth got bigger and it started to go around and around, faster and faster!

"Help!" Jack screamed.

What is going to happen next?

2 I don't believe you!

**Look at the pictures on pages 7 and 8.
Who can you see? Where are they?**

Jack and Miss Williams heard loud bangs outside the phone booth and they saw bright lights.

"Where are we? What's happening?" Jack asked nervously.

Miss Williams looked at Jack. "It works!" she said happily. "It works!"

"What works?" Jack asked.

"Alexander Graham Bell's big idea!" she answered. "Traveling in time!"

"What do you mean?" Jack asked.

"Bell lived a hundred years ago. He was a scientist who invented lots of things – like the telephone. One of his ideas was traveling in time," Miss Williams explained.

"Did you make this phone booth?" Jack asked quickly. He was very excited and very frightened at the same time.

"Yes," she said proudly. "And we are the first people to travel in time."

"Where are we going?" Jack asked

"I don't know," Miss Williams said. "What number did you dial?"

6 **TIME TRAVEL**

"156-6079," Jack said.

"I see," Miss Williams said. "We're going back over 400 years! The first four numbers are the important ones – 1566."

"I don't believe you!" Jack said.

Suddenly there was a loud bang and the phone booth stopped going around.

"Here we are in 1566," Miss Williams said.

Miss Williams opened the door and looked out. Then she turned to Jack and said, "Come on! This must be 1566 but I don't think we are in Boston. We're in the garden of a palace!"

Jack followed her out of the phone booth into a garden full of trees and flowers. There were two other people in the garden. There was a man wearing a hat, and behind him

there was a tall red-haired woman.

"The palace looks like Holyrood Palace. We must be in Edinburgh," said Miss Williams.

"Wow! That's Mary, Queen of Scots!" Jack said.

"She's beautiful," Miss Williams said quietly. "And who's the man?" she asked.

"I'm not sure, but I think it's Lord Darnley, her husband," Jack answered.

"Look at Mary!" Miss Williams said suddenly.

Mary was behind her husband. There was a knife in her hand.

What is Mary going to do?

3 A magic gun

Look at the pictures on this page and on page 10. What is happening? Do Jack and Miss Williams escape?

"Stop!" Jack shouted at Mary Queen of Scots. But she didn't hear him. Her knife was close to Lord Darnley's back. He didn't know his wife was behind him.

"That wasn't loud enough," Jack said. "I must shout louder."

"No," Miss Williams said. "Don't! You shouldn't change history."

"But she's going to kill him," Jack said. "I must stop her." And again he shouted "Stop!"

Mary turned and looked in surprise. She saw a teenage boy and an old woman with white hair. Their clothes were unusual. Mary's knife fell to the ground and she kicked it into the grass. Lord Darnley turned around and saw Mary. She smiled and took his hand.

"Who are these people?" Lord Darnley asked.

"I don't know," Mary answered angrily. "But they shouldn't be here."

Some soldiers ran up and they had guns in their hands.

"Wait!" Miss Williams shouted to the soldiers. "Don't come any closer or I'll fire my magic gun."

Then she took a flashlight out of her pocket, and flashed the light in the soldiers' eyes.

"Aah!" they screamed and their guns fell to the ground.

Miss Williams and Jack ran back to the phone booth. "Let's go back to the present," Miss Williams said.

It was dark in the phone booth. Jack dialed 1999. Lights flashed, there was a loud bang, and the phone booth started

to go around and around.

"Wow!" Jack said. "We escaped! And Mary didn't kill Darnley. I stopped her."

"Now listen to me," Miss Williams said a little angrily. "Let me tell you the first rule of time travel. You mustn't try to change history. Darnley will die next year – in 1567."

"OK," Jack said. "The flashlight was a clever idea, Miss Williams."

"Thank you, Jack. I think you can call me Jenny," Miss Williams said with a smile, "as we are the first time travelers."

There was a loud bang and more flashes of light.

"Here we are," Jenny said. "Back in the present. Open the door, Jack."

Jack opened the door a little sadly, because he was sorry that the journey was over. But when he looked out, he had a surprise. The light outside the phone booth was very bright and the air was hot. There was yellow sand everywhere, and he couldn't see any people.

"Oh, no!" he said. "I think I dialed 2999, not 1999! We're in the future!"

What will life in 2999 be like?

10 TIME TRAVEL

4 I've just seen a monster

**Look at the picture on this page.
What has happened to the world?**

"Jack, what have you done?" Jenny asked.

"I'm sorry Miss, er, Jenny. I've made a mistake," Jack said. "I've taken us 1000 years into the future."

Jenny laughed. "Never mind! I've always wanted to know what the future will be like. Now we can see."

They stepped out of the phone booth and looked around. At first all they could see was yellow sand.

"Where are we?" Jack asked.

"Look, there's the Statue of Liberty," Jenny said. "We must be in New York City."

Jack could only see the top of the statue. All around it was sand. "What's happened?" he asked.

Jenny looked at him. "Don't you remember anything from your science lessons? About saving the environment and not wasting energy?"

"So you mean that people have used up all the energy," Jack said.

"And they've polluted the environment," Jenny said. "Now there's nothing left. Just the sea and sand."

TIME TRAVEL 11

"How awful!" Jack said. "And there's nothing we can do about it."

"Oh yes, there is," said Jenny with a big smile. "We can go back to the present and tell people. We'll tell people what the future will be like. Then perhaps they'll listen and save the earth."

"But you said we mustn't change the past when we're time traveling," Jack said.

"That's right," Jenny said. "But we can change the future because it hasn't happened! Now let's get the phone booth ready for the journey."

"How does the phone booth work?" Jack asked.

"It uses energy from the sun," she explained. "The roof is saving the sun's energy. Soon we'll be ready to go."

Jack sat in the sand and waited. Then he saw something interesting. "Look," he said. "Down by the sea. There's something moving."

Jenny looked. There was a thing coming out of the water. "It's nothing," she said, and went back into the phone booth.

Jack watched. The thing started to move across the sand towards them. It was like a long snake, 20 or 30 meters long, with a very thick body. Then it disappeared under the sand.

12 TIME TRAVEL

Five minutes later, the sand near the phone booth started to move. A huge head with a big mouth came up out of the sand. It was the snake, and it was only a few meters away!

Jack was scared. He ran into the phone booth and closed the door. "Jenny, I've just seen a monster!"

Then there was a knocking noise outside the phone booth.

"The snake's body is around the phone booth!" Now Jack was really frightened. "We can't escape!"

**Will the snake get Jack and Jenny?
What can they do to escape?**

5 It's dead now

Look at the pictures on this page and on page 15. What has happened to the snake? Have Jack and Jenny escaped?

"I can't start the time machine," Jenny said. "The snake is too heavy."

"What are we going to do?" Jack asked.

Jenny smiled. "The time machine is made of a special metal. When I press this button," Jenny showed Jack a small blue button on the side of the phone, "the outside of the phone booth gets hotter and hotter. So if the snake stays there, it fries!"

She pressed the button. Nothing happened for a minute or two. Then there was an awful smell, and blue smoke came in under the door. Suddenly there was a terrible scream outside the phone booth.

"It's dead now," Jenny said brightly. "Do you want to see it?"

"No, thank you," said Jack. It was hot in the phone booth and his face was red. "Let's go now."

"OK," Jenny said. "When do you want to go?"

"What do you mean?" Jack asked. "When? Surely you mean 'Where'?"

"No," said Jenny. "This is a time machine – it travels through time. So 'When do you want to go?' means 'What time would you like to travel to?'."

"I see," Jack said. "I'd like to go back to the present."

"Right." Jenny dialed 1999 and there were the usual bangs and flashes of light.

"Jenny," Jack asked. "How does the time machine work?"

"It's really very simple," she said. "It uses energy from the sun in a laser. When you dial the year on the phone, the laser makes a small explosion and we travel through time."

"But why don't we stay in Boston?" asked Jack.

"Because the Earth is always turning. When we traveled to the past, the Earth moved under us so we landed across the Atlantic Ocean. When we traveled to the future, the Earth turned all the way around so we landed in New York," said Miss Williams.

"Let's travel back to the present and see if we can land in Boston. I'm hungry!"

Suddenly there were two loud bangs, louder than usual. The time machine stopped and then started again in a great flash of light. Then it finally stopped.

"We've arrived," Jenny said. "Welcome back to 1999!"

Jack carefully opened the door of the time machine and looked out. He turned to Jenny.

14 **TIME TRAVEL**

"We're back," he said. "But it isn't 1999!"

They stepped out of the time machine and looked around. They were on Arlington Street, near the Boston Common, a large park.

"You're right," Jenny said. "It's earlier than 1999, but not a lot earlier. Why didn't the time machine stop in 1999? I dialed the right number."

"I know why!" Jack answered. "Look at the roof of the phone booth!"

**What has happened to the time machine?
Where are Jack and Jenny?**

6 If you don't get a job, I won't marry you

Look at the picture. What are Jack and Jenny doing? Who do you think the people on the next seat are?

On the roof of the phone booth there was a long thing. It was part of the dead monster. It slowly fell off the roof onto the ground, and it melted into water.

"The monster was interfering with the machine. That's why we've come back to the wrong date," Jenny said.

"But what date is it?" Jack asked.

"Let's go and find out," Jenny said.

"But is it safe to leave the time machine here?" Jack asked. "What if someone takes it and we can't go back to 1999?"

"Don't be silly," Jenny said. "It looks just like an ordinary phone booth. No one will notice it."

"Let's get some food," Jack said. "I'm starving. I'd love a pizza."

They walked along Arlington Street, but they couldn't find a pizza restaurant.

Jenny went up to a man who was selling newspapers. "Excuse me," she said. "Where can I get a pizza?"

"A piece of what?" the man asked.

"You know," Jenny said. "Pizza – Italian food."

"I don't know what you mean," the man said. "But if you want food, there's a seafood restaurant in the next street."

"How strange!" Jack thought. "He doesn't know what a pizza is!"

"Look!" Jenny pointed at the newspapers. All the front pages said: "Man on the Moon" and the date was July 21, 1969.

"Thirty years ago!" Jack said.

They bought some fried clams and French fries and ate them in the park next to Arlington Street. A young man and

16 TIME TRAVEL

woman were sitting on the next seat. The woman was 17 or 18 and had short blond hair. The man was a little older, with long hair and glasses, and he was holding a guitar.

"I've seen those two before!" Jack said quietly.

The man and woman were having an argument.

"If you don't get a job, I won't marry you!" the woman shouted.

"I know that voice," Jack said. "That's my mother's voice."

"And who's the man?" Jenny asked.

"I think it's my father," Jack said. "But he looks strange with long hair."

"If you say that once more, I'll never speak to you again," the man shouted to the woman.

"Get a job!" the woman shouted back. "And stop playing that guitar. You're not one of the Beatles, you know."

"Right!" the man said. "Goodbye. You won't see me

again!" He stood up and walked away. The woman started to cry.

"Quick! Do something, Jack," Jenny said.

"Why?" Jack asked. "It's nothing to do with me."

"Oh, yes, it is," Jenny said. "If your parents don't get married, you won't be born!"

What do you think Jack is going to do?

7 We've left Jenny behind!

Look at the picture. Why is Jack running after the bus?

Jack was shocked. "You mean that if my parents don't get married, I won't exist?"

"Yes," Jenny said. "I know I said you shouldn't interfere with history. But this is different. This is your own life. Run after your father and bring him back. I'll talk to your mother."

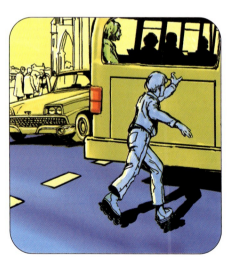

Jack nodded.

"You'll have to be quick!" Jenny said.

"I have an idea!" Jack ran over to the time machine. His rollerblades were on the floor. He quickly put them on and went after his father. There were lots of people on Arlington Street and they stopped to look at Jack.

"What on earth

18 **TIME TRAVEL**

does he have on his feet? I've never seen anything like it," someone said. "He's going so fast."

Then Jack saw his father – and he was getting on a bus! Jack went as fast as he could and followed the bus along Arlington Street. When the bus stopped at the end of the street, Jack's father got off, and Jack went up to him.

"Excuse me," Jack said.

His father looked at Jack's clothes and the rollerblades.

"Hello," his father said. "Who are you? What do you want?"

"It's ... it's ..." Jack didn't know what to say.

"Is this some kind of joke?" Jack's father asked. "Are you an actor or something?"

"No," Jack explained. "You see, it's like this. I was walking in the park on Arlington Street a minute ago ..."

"Walking?" Jack's father said, "With those things on your feet?"

"And a woman asked me to give you a message. She had short blond hair and her name was Kathy," Jack said.

It wasn't true about the message but he had to say something.

"And what was the message?" Jack's father asked.

Jack breathed in deeply. "She's sorry. She didn't mean what she said. She doesn't want to change you. Please come back."

"Really?" Jack's father smiled. "Where is she now?"

"In the park," Jack said.

"OK, thank you." Jack's father started to walk quickly back toward the park. Jack followed him on his rollerblades. But when they got back to the park, Kathy wasn't there. Jenny was sitting alone on the seat.

"Have you seen a woman with blond hair?" Jack's father asked Jenny.

"Yes," she answered. "She's just left. I felt sorry for her. She was crying."

"Where did she go? I have to see her," Jack's father said.
"She was going home," Jenny said.
"I'll call her," Jack's father said.
He walked to the phone booth and closed the door.
"Oh no!" Jenny and Jack said at the same time.

Jack rollerbladed over to the phone booth and opened the door. But it was too late. Jack's father was already dialing. The door closed behind Jack. He and his father were in the phone booth together. There was a bang and a flash of light, and the phone booth started to turn around.

"Oh no!" Jack said. "We've left Jenny behind!"

What are Jack and his father going to do?
What is Jenny going to do?

8 This is amazing!

Look at the picture on page 21. What year is it?
Why are the girls looking at the man?

"What's happening?" Jack's father asked. He sounded frightened.

"It's hard to explain," Jack said. "And if I do explain, you won't believe me. What number did you dial?"

"Kathy's number," Jack's father said. "199-9632."

"Great!" Jack said." We're going back to the present!"

"What did you say?" Jack's father asked.

"I said we were going back to the present, to 1999," Jack replied with a big smile.

"I don't know what you're talking about," Jack's father said. "And why won't this door open?"

There was a bang and a big flash of light.

"Now you can open the door," Jack said. "You're going to get a surprise!"

20 **TIME TRAVEL**

Jack's father opened the door. They were on Arlington Street in 1999.

"You told me I was going to get a surprise," Jack's father said. "But this is amazing!"

"Have a quick look around," Jack said. "Then we're going back to 1969 again. Kathy's waiting for you."

Jack and his father stepped out of the time machine. Two girls, who were walking past, stopped and looked at them.

"Hey," one of them said to Jack. "Hi! Jack." It was Tracy from Jack's class at school.

"Who's your friend?" Tracy asked. "He looks just like one of the Beatles."

"Yeah," Tracy's friend said. "Look at his hair and those glasses. Just like John Lennon's."

"Perhaps it is John Lennon," Tracy said. "He has a guitar."

"Don't be silly," Jack said. He didn't want people to notice his father. He wanted to go back to 1969 as quickly as possible. "John Lennon's dead."

"Who is he then?" Tracy asked. "If he isn't John Lennon."

"He's my father," Jack said without thinking.

"No, I'm not," Jack's father said. "I've never seen you before in my life."

"Don't tell lies, Jack," Tracy said. "He's only a few years older than you. He can't be your father."

"It's John Lennon," Tracy's friend said. She started shouting, "Look everyone! It's John Lennon!"

Soon more people came to look at Jack and his father.

"I said you were an actor," Jack's father said to Jack. "Is this a play? Why are they all wearing funny clothes? And John Lennon's alive, he isn't dead."

"Come on," Jack said. "We can't stay here." He took his father's arm and pulled him into the phone booth. Tracy and her friends followed and stood around the booth.

"Why are you making a phone call now?" Jack's father asked. "I'd like to talk to those girls."

"No," Jack replied. "The only girl you're going to talk to is Kathy."

Jack dialed 1969. Nothing happened.

What do you think is wrong with the time machine? How will Jack and his father rescue Jenny?

9 You're just in time!

**Look at the picture on page 24.
Who is in the time machine? Where is it going?**

Tracy opened the door of the phone booth.

"John Lennon, come and play for us." She pulled Jack's father out of the phone booth. He sat down on the grass and started to play a Beatles song.

Jack listened to his father. He felt proud of him because he played quite well. Then he thought about Jenny, still there in 1969.

"Why won't the time machine work?" Jack asked himself. "Perhaps it doesn't have any power? Jenny said it used the sun's energy." But it was cloudy and there wasn't any sunshine.

Now there was a large crowd of people around his father. Everyone was trying to listen to the person they thought was

John Lennon. Then Jack noticed a car from the local TV station. A woman and a man got out with a TV camera and started to push through the crowd.

"Do you want the lights?" the man asked.

"No," the woman replied. "There are too many people here."

Jack had an idea. He went over to the car and saw two strong lights in the back. He looked around. Everyone was listening to his father. Jack took the lights out of the car and carried them over to the phone booth. He put the lights on the roof of the booth and turned them on. Soon the time machine was ready to leave, and Jack put the lights back in the car.

Then he heard a police car and saw the flashing blue light on its roof. Two police officers got out and went into the crowd. A minute later they returned with Jack's father. "You can't perform here," one of the police officers said. But the crowd was angry and tried to stop the police.

"Hey," Jack said to the police officer, "Why don't you put him in the phone booth? He'll be safe there."

"Good idea!" the police officer said.

Jack quickly followed his father into the phone booth and dialed 1969. With a flash and a bang the time machine disappeared.

"What? Where have they gone?" the police said.

Inside the time machine, Jack was talking angrily to his father.

"You're impossible," he said. "Why don't you do what I tell you? Now we're going back to 1969. You're going to talk to Kathy. And you're going to get married! OK?"

"But who ...?" Jack's father began.

"Don't ask any questions," Jack said. There was a flash and a bang. "We're here now!"

Jack and his father stepped out of the time machine. Jenny was waiting for them.

"You're just in time!" she said. "Here's Kathy."

Jack's father ran up to Kathy and put his arm around her.

"It"s time for us to go," Jenny said. She and Jack got into the time machine. "Dial 1999," said Jenny. Jack dialed and a woman's voice answered the phone! "Hello? Fire, police or ambulance?"

"Oh no!" said Jack. "I've dialed 911 by mistake!"

Jenny took the phone. "Sorry," she said. "Wrong number!"

**What do you think will happen to Jack and Jenny?
Will they get back to 1999 safely?
Or will they travel to other times?
What time would you like to travel to? Why?**